This
Libra
w
lib

NATURE UNLEASHED

FLOODS

Louise and Richard Spilsbury

FRANKLIN WATTS
LONDON • SYDNEY

Franklin Watts
First published in Great Britain in 2017 by The Watts Publishing Group

Credits
Series Editors: Sarah Eason and Harriet McGregor
Series Designer: Simon Borrough
Picture Researcher: Rachel Blount

Picture credits: Cover: Dept of Defense: U.S. Coast Guard photograph by Petty Officer 2nd Class Kyle Niemi; Inside: NASA: Jacques Descloitres, MODIS Land Team 25; Shutterstock: Asianet-Pakistan 11, Paolo Costa 19c, Emattil 6–7, Sohel Parvez Haque 1, Jejim 23, Pius Lee 7, Dusan Milenkovic 4–5, Naveeen 17, IR Stone 15r; Wikimedia Commons: Edu Alarcón 19t, Histed/Ernest Walter/1862-1947 13, Pieter Kuiper/Agency for International Development/National Archives 15l, Leruswing 27, Archival Photography by Steve Nicklas, NOS, NGS 9, Airman 1st Class Cheryl Sanzi (USAF) 21.

Every attempt has been made to clear copyright. Should there be any inadvertent omission please apply to the publisher for rectification.

HB ISBN: 978 1 4451 5397 1

Printed in China

Franklin Watts
An imprint of
Hachette Children's Group
Part of The Watts Publishing Group
Carmelite House
50 Victoria Embankment
London EC4Y 0DZ

An Hachette UK Company
www.hachette.co.uk

www.franklinwatts.co.uk

Contents

FLOOD DANGER

When a flood brings water crashing onto land that is normally dry, it causes chaos. It washes away people, cars and trees, and buries homes under mud. It ruins fields of crops and damages or destroys bridges and roads.

How Dangerous?

Some places experience local floods. Water from a river may overflow, washing shallow water onto streets. Other floods are huge and last for weeks. The flood waters can kill people, wash away possessions, knock down power lines and cause fires. The dirt in flood waters can also **pollute** drinking water supplies and cause disease.

Measuring Disaster

Scientists are trying to work out how to predict floods and give people time to **evacuate** and reach higher ground or another safe place.

Floods happen when large clouds bring heavy rain. → People use **satellite** images taken from high above the Earth's surface to see where rain clouds are going.

Some clouds bring more rain than others. → Scientists use **radar** to detect how much moisture, or water droplets, there is in a cloud and whether it is in the form of rain or snow.

Floods happen when land cannot absorb water, for example, in areas of dried mud. → Scientists study land and make computer models and maps to show where floods are more likely to happen.

In 2014, heavy rains caused catastrophic flooding and mudslides, which destroyed the town of Krupanj in central Serbia.

Natural disasters have taken place since the Earth was formed. People have many ways of deciding what the world's worst natural disasters have been, from the deadliest disaster to the costliest. This book includes some of the worst flood disasters in history.

FLOODS IN ACTION

Floods are one of the most common natural disasters in the world. They usually happen in places where flat, low-lying land borders rivers, lakes or seas.

Rainwater washes more quickly down a slope without trees.

Rising Waters

When the level of the water in a river, lake or sea rises, it spills out over the land. Several factors contribute to floods. Heavy rains can swell rivers. A storm can force seawater higher up the shore. **Cyclones** and **hurricanes** can bring sudden downpours and earthquakes can cause large waves of water to wash onto the coast. Flash floods are floods that happen very suddenly after a storm.

Where Floods Happen

Floods can happen almost anywhere. In the United Kingdom, floods usually happen in spring and autumn, when there is more rain. **Tropical** countries, such as India, have rainy and dry seasons. The **monsoon** season is when winds carrying moisture from the warm ocean nearby bring months of heavy rain. In these regions there are regular and heavy floods during the monsoon season.

In some parts of the world such as China, floods happen regularly and bring rainwater that is essential for growing crops such as rice.

Problems

People can sometimes increase the risk of flooding in an area. **Dams** and **reservoirs** are built to store water but these can overflow after prolonged, heavy rain and flood out onto towns and villages downstream. When people cut down forests, wind blows the top layer of soil away. Then, when it rains, the water runs off the land instead of soaking in. When people build roads and cover land in hard surfaces, there is even less soil to absorb rainwater.

10 MISSISSIPPI

The Great Mississippi Flood of 1927 is the biggest flood in US history and one of the worst ever natural disasters in the United States. It also became famous for the way some people in the worst-hit town, Greenville, treated the African-Americans among them.

UNITED STATES

Greenville ●

Mississippi

A River's Power

Along the Mississippi Valley in 1927, rain fell in quantities that exceeded the yearly average by ten or more times. Even though **tributaries** were overflowing, people in Greenville still felt safe because the US Army Corps of Engineers had built **levees** to keep back the Mississippi River. The engineers had assured people that the levees would hold. Unfortunately, everyone underestimated the river's power.

On the Record

African-American **plantation** workers were forced to pile sand bags on top of the levees to reinforce them. When the levees broke, many workers were washed away and thousands were stranded for days without food or water.

The first levee broke on 16 April then another on 21 April. Over the next few weeks, all the levees collapsed, one after the other. Water poured through gaps and onto the streets.

It took more than two months for the flood waters to completely subside.

In total, more than 60,000 **square kilometres** (sq km) of land was submerged, hundreds of thousands of people were made homeless and around 250 people died.

In some places, homes were buried under 9 metres (m) of water. Tens of thousands of people were stranded on rooftops or left clinging to trees.

9 PAKISTAN

The River Indus in Pakistan flooded in late July and early August 2010. This natural disaster is considered to be one of the worst in the country's history.

Pakistan

Monsoon Floods

The floods were caused by record-breaking monsoon rains. Monsoon winds bring heavy rain to parts of Southeast Asia from May to September. They often cause floods but not usually on a massive scale. In 2010, the River Indus overflowed and broke through flood defences. The floodwaters washed away roads, bridges, and submerged large areas of land. Almost 2,000 people were killed. An international relief effort helped to rebuild the worst-hit areas, and flood agencies are working to provide better flood forecasting in the future.

On the Record

At its worst, the flood covered around one-fifth of Pakistan's land in water and affected almost 20 million people.

The floods damaged or destroyed 1.6 million homes, leaving 14 million people with nowhere to live.

Rescuers struggled to reach people stranded by rising waters or cut off because roads and bridges were damaged. The army used helicopters to airlift people to safety.

The floods that swept over the land left millions hungry and in danger of catching diseases from the dirty water.

The floods destroyed 22,000 sq km of crops; 450,000 farm animals were killed.

8 JOHNSTOWN

The Johnstown Flood of 1889 was the deadliest flood in US history. The South Fork Dam burst and the flood waters' raging torrent almost wiped the town of Johnstown from existence, killing 2,209 people.

UNITED STATES

Johnstown

The Death of a Dam

The area around Johnstown, Pennsylvania, in the United States had received a lot of heavy rain, which filled the reservoir behind the South Fork Dam, 23 kilometres (km) upstream of the town. The dam was built from layers of soil and was not in a good state of repair, even though it held back a large volume of water. The town was warned that the dam might give way, but there had been several false alarms, so tragically the warnings were ignored.

On the Record

The dam broke on the afternoon of 31 May. It released a 9-m-high wall of water, which raced down the valley towards Johnstown at speeds of up to 32–64 kilometres per hour (kph).

In Johnstown, 18 million tonnes of water full of trees, rocks and **debris** crashed into the streets. The flood flattened everything in its path and washed away steel mills, homes, farm animals and people.

The flood was stopped by a huge stone bridge on the far side of the town. This caused water and all of the debris in it, such as trains, wood and human bodies, to pile up behind it.

Around 10 sq km of Johnstown were completely destroyed.

Wooden items trapped at the bridge caught fire and killed more people.

7 NORTH SEA

In 1953, a combination of high tides, strong winds and storm surges caused the North Sea to rise by almost six metres. It broke through flood defences and caused devastating floods in low-lying parts of the Netherlands, Belgium and the United Kingdom.

UNITED KINGDOM

NETHERLANDS
BELGIUM

North Sea

Storm Surges

A storm surge happens when an area of low **pressure** and high winds push an unusually high tide towards a coastline. When this water hits low-lying land, it floods the seashore. On the night of Saturday 31 January, 1953, and the morning of 1 February 1953, the already high **spring tides** of the North Sea swept ashore. No one was warned this would happen.

On the Record

The floods killed more than 2,000 people: 307 in England, 19 in Scotland and 1,800 in the Netherlands, where as much as 50 per cent of the land is less than 1 m above **sea level**.

More than 650 sq km of land was flooded with salty seawater, making it unfit for growing crops for several years. In the United Kingdom, large areas of East Anglia and the Thames Estuary flooded. In the Netherlands 10 per cent of all farmland was submerged.

The River Thames flood barrier

This view shows the damage the 1953 floods caused the town of Zuid Beveland in the Netherlands.

Today, the River Thames is protected from floods by the Thames Barrier. The Netherlands now has a series of impressive flood defences.

The floods caused about £50 million worth of damage, about £1.2 billion in today's money.

The flood damaged and destroyed power stations, gasworks, roads, railways, sewage services and water services.

6 NORTH INDIA

In June 2013, the mountainous region of Uttarakhand in northern India suffered days of heavy monsoon rains. The rains triggered devastating floods and landslides that killed more than 5,000 people.

Uttarakhand

North India

Human Impacts

The flood was made worse because of human activity. People had cut down forests in the valleys, so there were fewer tree roots to hold the soil together. Hydroelectric dams built across rivers caused water levels to rise. There were also many homes and hotels built on riverbanks and in other areas that were likely to flood. An international relief effort supported by the World Bank worked to rebuild the area. Unfortunately, new floods have caused further loss of life.

On the Record

The rain was so heavy that 59 centimetres (cm) fell in just two days.

Due to the heavy and persistent rain, a **glacier** in the mountains melted. It triggered flooding in the River Mandinkini.

On 16–17 June 2013, the floods washed away 400 villages, and roads, bridges and other **infrastructure** in 12 of the 13 districts in Uttarakhand.

This house in Kedarnath, Uttarakhand, was destroyed by a landslide following the 2013 floods.

Almost 100,000 pilgrims and tourists visiting Hindu mountain shrines and temples were stranded in the mountain valleys after bridges and roads were destroyed. Some were rescued by helicopter.

5 VENEZUELA

In December 1999, days of torrential rain finally took their toll and caused catastrophic flooding and landslides in the mountainous region of Vargas, in Venezuela. Between 10,000 and 30,000 people were killed in the disaster.

Venezuela

Vargas

Deadly Debris Flows

The heavy rains washed down the side of the Avila Mountain. The waters dislodged mud, rocks and large boulders. Together they formed deadly 'debris flows'. These stormed down the slopes towards towns and villages below, damaging or destroying everything in their path. Many people living in the area below the mountain were buried under the wet mud or washed into the sea. Ten years later, people were still living in partially collapsed buildings. Today inhabitants live in fear of further floods and landslides.

On the Record

This building in Vargas partially collapsed.

In Vargas, several hundred thousand people lived on the narrow strip of coastline at the base of steep mountains. The floods destroyed a 100-km stretch of the coastline.

The floods and debris flows began late on the night of 15 December and continued until the afternoon of 16 December.

The Avila Mountains rise to more than 2,500 m above sea level.

An estimated 190,000 people were evacuated and tens of thousands of people were made homeless.

Poor families suffered the most, because the torrents of mud and water swept away their lightly constructed homes and **shanty towns**. Entire blocks of flats collapsed.

Telephone, water, electricity and sewage services were destroyed or damaged.

19

4 BANGLADESH

During the monsoon season in 1974 heavy rains caused severe flooding in Bangladesh. People died in the floodwaters and from starvation after the floods devastated most of the rice and other crops in the area. The disaster led to the deaths of at least 28,000 people.

Bangladesh

Flood Plains

The monsoon season brings vital rainwater to Bangladesh for growing crops. The problem is that around three-quarters of the country is less than 10 m above sea level. Almost 80 per cent of the land is prone to flooding.

On the Record

The monsoon rains caused massive flooding in the River Brahmaputra, leaving around 40 per cent of the country under water.

The people who suffered most were the poor. Their houses collapsed or were submerged under water. The floods washed away their belongings.

Bangladesh is frequently affected by flooding. This village was completely destroyed by flood waters during a cyclone.

The flood damaged about 536,000 tonnes of crops. Food prices rose, so poorer people could not afford to eat.

The loss of crops meant many farm workers could not get jobs harvesting the crops. Without wages, they could not buy food for their families.

3 RIVER YANGTZE

The River Yangtze runs through central and eastern China. It is the longest river in Asia. Over time, the floods in this river have killed many thousands of people. One of the worst occurred in 1998.

CHINA

Three Gorges Dam

River Yangtze

A History of Flooding

Floods are one of the most serious natural disasters in China. During the twentieth century alone, the Yangtze experienced five disastrous floods. The flood of 1998 was not the deadliest. It killed around 4,000 people. However, it was devastating and record-breaking in other ways. The 1998 flood lasted more than 80 days and was one of the largest ever recorded.

To stop the River Yangtze from flooding, the Chinese government built the Three Gorges Dam (see below). Building work had begun in 1994 but was not able to prevent the 1998 flood. However, it did hold back the worst of a flood in 2010.

The 1998 floods began when unusually heavy rains fell from the start of June to the end of August. The volume of rainfall was up to twice as much as usual.

This is the Three Gorges Dam. To build it, the Chinese government had to remove 1.2 million people from their towns and villages before the land behind the dam disappeared under water.

The flood destroyed 13 million homes and submerged 100,000 sq km of land.

The flood made around 15 million people homeless.

2 GANGES DELTA

The Ganges Delta is an area of low-lying land about 355 km wide along the Bay of Bengal. It is where two huge rivers – the River Ganges in India and the River Brahmaputra in Bangladesh – meet the sea. In 1970, the area was hit by terrible floods.

INDIA

BANGLADESH

Ganges Delta

Bay of Bengal

Cyclone Storm

Cyclones regularly form over the warm seas of the Bay of Bengal between August and October, when weather in the region is hot. In November 1970, Cyclone Bhola blew in towards the Bay of Bengal. Unfortunately, the shape of the bay helped to funnel the cyclone towards the coastline. A huge storm surge approached the land. This sudden increase in sea level flooded the delta regions in both India and Bangladesh (known as East Pakistan at the time).

On the Record

Waves from the storm surge that flooded the delta were 8 m high.

Around 500,000 people died; most were drowned.

Survivors said the water made a roar like thunder as it raced towards them.

River Brahmaputra

Around 85 per cent of all homes in the area were destroyed or badly damaged. More than one million people were left homeless.

River Ganges

Bay of Bengal

Crops were destroyed and farm animals drowned throughout the region.

This aerial view shows the Ganges-Brahmaputra Delta, the area flooded in 1970.

1 CHINA

The flooding that happened across central China in 1931 was the deadliest natural disaster of the twentieth century. Between July and August that year there was a series of devastating floods when China's three main rivers – the Yangtze, the Yellow and the Huai – burst their banks.

Wuhan • • Nanjing

China

Deadliest Flood

In late summer 1931, there were increasingly heavy rains over parts of central China and a series of cyclones. The most destructive floods began in July and continued for two months. The death toll from the floods, and subsequent disease and famine, was between 850,000 and four million. The floods left more than 80 million people homeless.

On the Record

Many areas were covered in water up to 5 m deep for up to six months.

When the River Huai overflowed into the city of Nanjing, China's capital at that time, millions of people drowned. Many of those who survived later died from diseases such as cholera.

Water broke through the levees containing the Grand Canal and caused more floods. In one area, 20,000 people drowned in their sleep.

The water level rose 16 m in the area now known as Wuhan.

The Yellow River is named for the large amounts of fine yellow sediment that colour its water.

WHERE IN THE WORLD?

North Sea

This map shows the locations of the floods featured in this book.

River Yangtze

China

North India

Pakistan

Bangladesh

Ganges Delta

INDIAN OCEAN

Read the case studies about the Mississippi flood (1927), the number ten flood in this book, and the flood in China (1931), which is number one. How do they differ?

What facts can you find in this book to support the argument that human actions can make flood disasters worse?

Johnstown

Mississippi

ATLANTIC
OCEAN

PACIFIC
OCEAN

Venezuela

Why do floods happen? Describe in your own words some of the different causes of floods.

How can scientists predict where floods might happen?

GLOSSARY

crops plants grown for food

cyclones hurricanes that occur in the South Pacific Ocean and Indian Ocean

dams barriers built to hold back river water; hydroelectric dams are used to make electricity with the power of falling water

debris loose waste material

delta a roughly triangular area of land where slow-moving river water meets the sea

evacuate to get away from an area that is dangerous to somewhere that is safe

glacier a large, very slow-moving river of ice

hurricanes storms with violent winds and heavy rains

infrastructure structures such as roads and railways that towns and cities need

landslides collapses of masses of earth or rock from mountains or cliffs

levees raised walls or banks by a river, canal or sea designed to hold back floodwaters

monsoon seasonal wind that brings heavy rains in some tropical parts of the world

plantation a large farm where crops such as cotton are grown

pollute to make something dirty or poisonous

pressure the pushing force on the ground caused by the weight of the air; air pressure depends on temperature and wind

radar a machine that uses radio waves to detect where objects are

reservoirs artificial lakes where water is collected and stored, often behind dams

satellite object in space that travels around the Earth

sea level the average height of the sea's surface

shanty towns areas on the edges of cities where poor people live in small, very cheaply built houses

spring tides tides in which there is the greatest difference between high and low water

square kilometres area; 1 sq km is a square that has sides 1 km long

storm surges abnormal rises of water caused by storms

tributaries rivers or streams that flow into larger rivers

tropical the area of the Earth around the equator that is hot all year

FURTHER READING

Books

Floods (Natural Disasters), Chris Oxlade, Wayland

Raging Floods (Awesome Forces of Nature), Louise and Richard Spilsbury, Heinemann Library

Rain and Floods (Weatherwise), Patience Coster, Wayland

Websites

Download this pdf for full instructions on how to make your own flooding game:
www.cornwall.gov.uk/media/3625325/Environment-Agency-Flood-game-plus-instructions_A4.pdf

Scroll down the page for children's first-hand accounts of the 2016 Boxing Day floods in the United Kingdom at:
www.ngkids.co.uk/science-and-nature/uk-floods-kids-boxing-day

For lots of information on rivers and flooding visit:
www.primaryhomeworkhelp.co.uk/rivers/floods/index.htm

Note to parents and teachers
Every effort has been made by the Publisher to ensure that these websites contain no inappropriate or offensive material. However, because of the nature of the Internet, it is impossible to guarantee that the contents of these sites will not be altered. We strongly advise that Internet access is supervised by a responsible adult.

INDEX

These are the lists of contents for each title in *Nature Unleashed:*

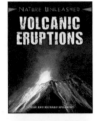

Volcanic Eruptions

Volcano Danger • Volcanoes in Action • Mount St. Helens • Pinatubo • El Chichón • Mount Vesuvius • Santa Maria • Nevado del Ruiz • Mount Pelee • Krakatau • Santorini • Mount Tambora • Where in the World? • Glossary • For More Information • Index

Earthquakes

Earthquake Danger • Earthquakes in Action • San Francisco, 1906 • Nepal, 2015 • Manjil-Rudbar, Iran, 1990 • Peru, 1970 • Kashmir, 2005 • Sichuan, 2008 • Japan, 1923 • Messina, Italy, 1908 • Tangshan, 1976 • Haiti ,2010 • Where in the World? • Glossary • For More Information • Index

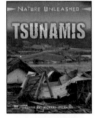

Tsunamis

Tsunami Danger • Tsunamis in Action • Flores Sea, Indonesia, 1992 • Chile, 1960 • Nankaido, Japan, 1946 • Tokaido, Japan 1923 • Papua New Guinea • San-Riku, Japan, 1933 • Andaman Sea-East Coast, 1941 • Moro Gulf, Philippines, 1976 • Japan, 2011 • Indian Ocean, 2004 • Where in the World? • Glossary • For More Information • Index

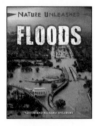

Floods

Flood Danger • Floods in Action • Mississippi Floods • Pakistan Floods, 2010 • Johnstown, 1889 • North Sea Floods, 1953 • North India Floods, 2013 • Vargas Tragedy, Venezuela, 1999 • Bangladesh, 1974 • Yangtse River Flood, 1998 • Ganges Delta, 1970 • Yellow River, China, 1931 • Where in the World? • Glossary • For More Information • Index

Hurricanes

Wind and Storm Danger • Tropical Storms in Action • Great Galveston Hurricane, 1900 • Typhoon Nina, 1975 • Hurricane Katrina, 2005 • Typhoon Bopha, 2012 • Hurricane Mitch, 1998 • Typhoon Tip, 1979 • Hurricane Camille, 1969 • Labor Day Hurricane, 1935 • Hurricane Patricia, 2015 • Typhoon Haiyan, 2013 • Where in the World? • Glossary • For More Information • Index

Wildfires

Fire Danger • Fires in Action • 2010 Russia • Ash Wednesday, 1983 • Landes Forest, 1949 • Black Saturday, 2009 • Miramichi, 1825 • Black Dragon, 1987 • Matheson Fire, 1916 • Cloquet Fire, 1918 • Peshtigo Fire, 1871 • Indonesia, 2015 • Where in the World? • Glossary • For More Information • Index